BEAGLES

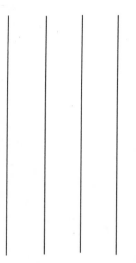

BEAGLES

Enthusiasm on four legs, beagles are famous for their voices, raised in chorus in pursuit of a fleeing hare.

Andrews and McMeel
© 1996 A. Eisen
Photo © 1996 I. Francais
All Rights Reserved.

Place
stamp
here

BEAGLES

BEAGLES

Enthusiasm on four legs, beagles are famous for their voices, raised in chorus in pursuit of a fleeing hare.

Andrews and McMeel
© 1996 A. Eisen
Photo © 1996 I. Français
All Rights Reserved.

Place stamp here

BEAGLES

BEAGLES

Enthusiasm on four legs, beagles are famous for their voices, raised in chorus in pursuit of a fleeing hare.

Andrews and McMeel
© 1996 A. Eisen
Photo © 1996 I. Français
All Rights Reserved.

Place
stamp
here

BEAGLES

Place stamp here

BEAGLES

Enthusiasm on four legs, beagles are famous for their voices, raised in chorus in pursuit of a fleeing hare.

Andrews and McMeel
© 1996 A. Eisen
Photo © 1996 I. François
All Rights Reserved.

BEAGLES

BEAGLES

Enthusiasm on four legs, beagles are famous for their voices, raised in chorus in pursuit of a fleeing hare.

Andrews and McMeel
© 1996 A. Eisen
Photo © 1996 I. Français
All Rights Reserved.

Place
stamp
here

BeaGLeS

BEAGLES

Enthusiasm on four legs, beagles are famous for their voices, raised in chorus in pursuit of a fleeing hare.

Andrews and McMeel
© 1996 A. Eisen
Photo © 1996 I. Français
All Rights Reserved.

Place
stamp
here

BEAGLES

BEAGLES

Enthusiasm on four legs, beagles are famous for their voices, raised in chorus in pursuit of a fleeing hare.

Andrews and McMeel
© 1996 A. Eisen
Photo © 1996 I. Français
All Rights Reserved.

Place
stamp
here

BEAGLES

BEAGLES

Enthusiasm on four legs, beagles are famous for their voices, raised in chorus in pursuit of a fleeing hare.

Andrews and McMeel
© 1996 A. Eisen
Photo © 1996 I. Français
All Rights Reserved.

Place
stamp
here

BEAGLES

BEAGLES

Enthusiasm on four legs, beagles are famous for their voices, raised in chorus in pursuit of a fleeing hare.

Andrews and McMeel
© 1996 A. Eisen
Photo © 1996 I. Français
All Rights Reserved.

Place
stamp
here

BeaGLeS

Place
stamp
here

BEAGLES

Enthusiasm on four legs, beagles are famous
for their voices, raised in chorus in pursuit
of a fleeing hare.

 Andrews and McMeel
© 1996 A. Eisen
Photo © 1996 I. Français
All Rights Reserved.

BEAGLES

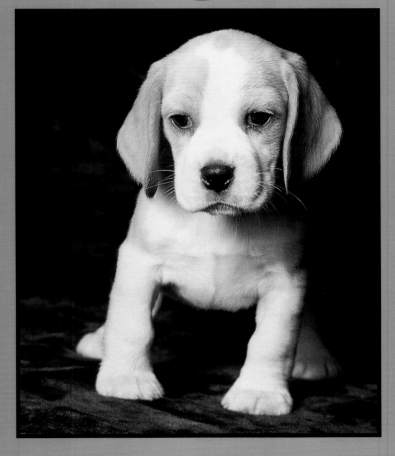

Place
stamp
here

BEAGLES

Enthusiasm on four legs, beagles are famous
for their voices, raised in chorus in pursuit
of a fleeing hare.

Andrews and McMeel
© 1996 A. Eisen
Photo © 1996 I. Français
All Rights Reserved.

BeaGLeS

BEAGLES

Enthusiasm on four legs, beagles are famous for their voices, raised in chorus in pursuit of a fleeing hare.

Andrews and McMeel
© 1996 A. Eisen
Photo © 1996 I. Français
All Rights Reserved.

Place stamp here

BEAGLES

Place
stamp
here

BEAGLES

Enthusiasm on four legs, beagles are famous
for their voices, raised in chorus in pursuit
of a fleeing hare.

Andrews and McMeel
© 1996 A. Eisen
Photo © 1996 I. François
All Rights Reserved.

BEAGLES

BEAGLES

Enthusiasm on four legs, beagles are famous for their voices, raised in chorus in pursuit of a fleeing hare.

Andrews and McMeel
© 1996 A. Eisen
Photo © 1996 I. Françcais
All Rights Reserved.

Place stamp here

BeaGLeS

Place stamp here

BEAGLES

Enthusiasm on four legs, beagles are famous for their voices, raised in chorus in pursuit of a fleeing hare.

Andrews and McMeel
© 1996 A. Eisen
Photo © 1996 I. Français
All Rights Reserved.

BEAGLES

BEAGLES

Enthusiasm on four legs, beagles are famous for their voices, raised in chorus in pursuit of a fleeing hare.

Andrews and McMeel
© 1996 A. Eisen
Photo © 1996 I. Français
All Rights Reserved.

Place
stamp
here

BEAGLES

BEAGLES

Enthusiasm on four legs, beagles are famous for their voices, raised in chorus in pursuit of a fleeing hare.

Andrews and McMeel
© 1996 A. Eisen
Photo © 1996 I. Français
All Rights Reserved.

Place stamp here

BEAGLES

BEAGLES

Enthusiasm on four legs, beagles are famous for their voices, raised in chorus in pursuit of a fleeing hare.

Andrews and McMeel
© 1996 A. Eisen
Photo © 1996 I. Français
All Rights Reserved.

Place
stamp
here

BEAGLES

BEAGLES

Enthusiasm on four legs, beagles are famous for their voices, raised in chorus in pursuit of a fleeing hare.

Andrews and McMeel
© 1996 A. Eisen
Photo © 1996 I. François
All Rights Reserved.

Place stamp here

BEAGLES

Place
stamp
here

BEAGLES

Enthusiasm on four legs, beagles are famous for their voices, raised in chorus in pursuit of a fleeing hare.

Andrews and McMeel
© 1996 A. Eisen
Photo © 1996 I. François
All Rights Reserved.

BeaGLeS

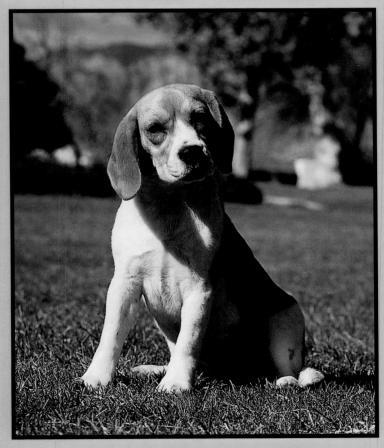

Place
stamp
here

BEAGLES

Enthusiasm on four legs, beagles are famous for their voices, raised in chorus in pursuit of a fleeing hare.

Andrews and McMeel
© 1996 A. Eisen
Photo © 1996 I. Français
All Rights Reserved.

BEAGLES

BEAGLES

Enthusiasm on four legs, beagles are famous for their voices, raised in chorus in pursuit of a fleeing hare.

Andrews and McMeel
© 1996 A. Eisen
Photo © 1996 I. François
All Rights Reserved.

BEAGLES

BEAGLES

Enthusiasm on four legs, beagles are famous for their voices, raised in chorus in pursuit of a fleeing hare.

Andrews and McMeel
© 1996 A. Eisen
Photo © 1996 I. Français
All Rights Reserved.

Place
stamp
here

BEAGLES

BEAGLES

Enthusiasm on four legs, beagles are famous for their voices, raised in chorus in pursuit of a fleeing hare.

Andrews and McMeel
© 1996 A. Eisen
Photo © 1996 I. Français
All Rights Reserved.

Place
stamp
here

BEAGLES

BEAGLES

Enthusiasm on four legs, beagles are famous for their voices, raised in chorus in pursuit of a fleeing hare.

Andrews and McMeel
© 1996 A. Eisen
Photo © 1996 I. Français
All Rights Reserved.

Place
stamp
here

BEAGLES

Place
stamp
here

BEAGLES

Enthusiasm on four legs, beagles are famous for their voices, raised in chorus in pursuit of a fleeing hare.

Andrews and McMeel
© 1996 A. Eisen
Photo © 1996 I. Français
All Rights Reserved.

BEAGLES

BEAGLES

Enthusiasm on four legs, beagles are famous for their voices, raised in chorus in pursuit of a fleeing hare.

Andrews and McMeel
© 1996 A. Eisen
Photo © 1996 I. Français
All Rights Reserved.

Place
stamp
here

BEAGLES

BEAGLES

Enthusiasm on four legs, beagles are famous
for their voices, raised in chorus in pursuit
of a fleeing hare.

Andrews and McMeel
© 1996 A. Eisen
Photo © 1996 I. François
All Rights Reserved.

Place
stamp
here

BEAGLES

Place
stamp
here

BEAGLES

Enthusiasm on four legs, beagles are famous for their voices, raised in chorus in pursuit of a fleeing hare.

Andrews and McMeel
© 1996 A. Eisen
Photo © 1996 I. Français
All Rights Reserved.